WHEN SUNDAY LOOKS LIKE TUESDAY:

Growing a Strong Faith for Everyday Living

JUDY CHATHAM

authorHOUSE®

AuthorHouse™
1663 Liberty Drive
Bloomington, IN 47403
www.authorhouse.com
Phone: 833-262-8899

Published by AuthorHouse   08/27/2021

ISBN: 978-1-6655-3221-1 (sc)
ISBN: 978-1-6655-3219-8 (hc)
ISBN: 978-1-6655-3220-4 (e)

Library of Congress Control Number: 2021914682

DEDICATED TO MY FAMILY

SOMETIMES WE FEEL LIKE SUNDAY LOOKS MORE LIKE TUESDAY. IN OUR FAMILY TUESDAY became 'CLINIC DAY' WHERE WE HEARD THE WORK SITUATION HAD CHANGED, WHERE WE LEARNED IF CHEMOTHERAPY WAS WORKING, WHERE WE HAD THE SERIOUS SURGERY, WHERE WE HAD THE UNEXPECTED FUNERAL, THE FAMILY FARM SALE AND MORE....

Clinic Day could bring a variety of activities, such as a spinal tap or a bone-marrow test, an evaluation of double vision or a myelogram. Plus, Tuesday could become 'drip day' for several hours of non-FDA-approved slow IV drip of a chemotherapy drug. But then, for us and thousands of others, Tuesday could bleed into every day of the week, making Sunday not feel like itself. And—'Thanking God for Friday' isn't likely to happen because a long weekend without access to medical care becomes more concerning than a long week with medical care.

That is why everyone in every situation, including you, dear reader, needs a strong faith for living the everyday life.

Will I persevere and stay the course to the end? Am I going to be tough enough for what comes my way? These were the words we heard during the Pandemic of 2020 and 2021. Oh, how we wanted the record to show our hard-nosed toughness.

John Steinbeck wrote *The Moon Is Down,* in which he described how people who had never before taken leadership roles, rose up and with grit and determination led the whole community out of extreme hardship. The reader sees that would-be leaders shrunk back, and the shy, quiet ones stepped up and led.

We could conclude from this surprising stepping up of the new leaders in Steinbeck's book that not even the person knows how strong she or he could be until the heat and pressure of the moment is on. There are times where there is little resource to train and plan for what comes our way.

Yet when people are cornered and desperate, mobilization will be immediate when that one strong, committed person steps up and moves the entire community to action and escape.

Certainly, there are principles associated with such leadership, whether in good times or in times of trouble, principles that educators have set forth for their students since public education began. Plus, Grandpa's wise practices concerning survival, and folk medicines and remedies from Grandma have been afloat for centuries. Like everything else, God put those tools and principles into our elders for teaching and training us. However, all such teachings aside, there is one practice Christians use that governs their way out of tight, smoldering, smothering, misery-laden places. That practice—one rests on God-inspired faith. Christians lean into their faith which is based on God's promises and never-ending presence in their lives. The Christian believes that God is in control and will lead them through it all.

BOOT CAMP FOR CREATIVE FAITH-BUILDING:

The definition of faith for many Christians comes from Book of Hebrews, chapter 11, in which the founding fathers and mothers of faith are listed. Through this listing, faith is defined:

Faith is confidence, often based upon past experiences, that God's new and fresh surprises will surely be ours.

Faith says God is who he says he is, that He created the world and everything in it. He is able to heal everything that has broken since that Creation, and he will do all he has promised.

Faith reminds us of our great heritage, that cloud of witnesses that surround us.

Faith reminds us that we are not God, and because of that fact, there will be things we will never completely understand, nor need to understand.

Faith imagines God beside us holding us up, being with us in compassion and assurance.

Faith says we know God keeps time differently than we do; therefore, he will do what he has promised in his perfect time.

Faith says God makes no mistakes whereas well-educated mortals sometimes do make mistakes.

Faith does not advise unreasonable actions; it is reasonable, but to a point. We understand that no one can know all that God knows.

Faith says it is likely we will die before we receive all that God has promised, but it will come to pass even after we have passed on. In the distance it will happen and that will be enough.

As far as we can comprehend, faith clarifies that bad things happen because we live in a fallen world. When the world is broken, we can be broken too.

Faith assures us that our faith and values are on a collision course in this world. Therefore, there may be crashes, and we may be involved, but God is with us and he is in control.

Christians say they live by faith and not by sight. II Corinthians 5:7. For instance, they might suppress the negative statistics of their disease and enhance the faith they have. They know that when living by faith, one does not rely on statistics. Some can see beyond the trial to the lessons learned and the growth they obtain from that trial.

Because of the strength of Christian claims and testimonies of how faith in God works, it is appropriate and encouraged for one to look into faith-building the Christian way.

One can only be certain of what she has lived, has seen first-hand. A skeptic could easily question general faith-building steps. That is—until that skeptic hears the testimony of someone who has been with Jesus through a trial.

In my own life, I had an upcoming medical test, an MRI, which I dreaded. Like the woman who once said, "Oh, I know I have Parkinson's disease, just pray for me to survive the MRI needed to diagnose it," I saw the MRI as a greater trial than the disease.

All issues aside, I include this MRI story here to show that one by one, year after year, one piles up a stack of faith-builders. Then the seeker weaves them together and

3

holds them tightly when she faces a crisis. With these resources at hand, that seeker can say, "I know this is serious business, but I remember the other times when I faced the same, and God walked with me through it all."

Laugh with me as we look at a woman (me) who has been faith-building all of her life, but, even with all of that living and learning, can look away 'for a moment' and forget that God never leaves, never forgets our dreaded appointments, and can be trusted to be with us through it all.

THE MRI ACCOUNT

I attended a publishing conference several years ago when a Christian leader and author opened his early afternoon remarks with a description of his experiences inside the tube of an MRI imaging chamber. His ice-breaker MRI story provided a light touch to the afternoon as we laughed at his description inside the 'torture' tube.

I had had my own MRI five years earlier. The experience was so memorable I had cautioned the technician to special handle my images because I would never be able to go headfirst into that tube again. Like many others in the room, I was recalling thoughts of 'tight places' as he described his story. Certainly, the funniest part of the account was the expression on his wild-eyed face as he talked.

Fast forward almost a decade later and my undiagnosed vertigo was giving me problems when I was invited to update my former MRI, but this time with an open-sided imaging machine. While the machine, the assistance and explanation may have been greatly improved, I could not imagine it that way. Now it was possible to look out the sides and see the technician exit the room leaving me with 5,000 pounds of steel inches from my face. All of this real or imagined weight would fall apart crushing my head at any part of my 30- minute procedure.

However, the combo of the self-diagnosed Meniere's disease and threat-of-the- coronavirus made me desperate enough to agree to another MRI...scheduled for a July/ Thursday morning at 7:30 sharp.

For this occasion, I had started praying the preceding Sunday with prayers focused on...'Dear God, help me live beyond Thursday morning.'

Between prayers that Sunday, I was preparing my house for my demise on Thursday. Tossing half-read papers, I came upon a devotional that had been sent to me as an advertisement for subscription. It was the daily dated kind that makes one feel guilty if it hasn't been read on the date intended. I quickly read the titles and came upon "The Pillow Jack." Scanning it, I soon knew why I had stopped to read it, for at the end was the author's name---JFG.

Jean and I, both small town newspaper columnists and dreamers of writing the world-changing Christian book had traveled together to writer's conferences, starting in Dallas in 118-degree temperature and continuing around the country for near to a decade of writing/speaking instruction. Together we had renamed one of her writings, mourned through family sorrows and laughed through her tugging her 'Big Bertha' suitcase through the terminals.

Years had passed; she had moved to new locations; her husband had died. Somehow during those changes we had lost touch with one another.

God had directed me to 'The Pillow Jack.' With 31 meditations, I chose this one.

This divine appointed mini-reunion with Jean had told me that God was nearby and guiding me through to Thursday. He was even helping me recall special memories in the mix.

Monday, I continued my purge of unnecessary things my family would have to deal with after my passing. Having been one of the ones to sort through the households of two sets of parents, I knew about the difficult task. As I worked, I was spurred on knowing I would surely have a heart attack during the MRI on Thursday.

On Monday evening I looked at the stack of mail my husband had brought in. On top I saw the name Marita in the return address on a personal note. All I needed to know was that one part of the name—Marita. My dear friend and mentor Florence Littauer, age 94, was now living with her daughter Marita. After steeling myself to open the note, I read that Florence had died two weeks earlier. Due to the Pandemic of 2020, the family held a small funeral, and she would be buried in Massachusetts at the family plot at a later date.

Florence, dear Florence! I could see all of her students, friends, and protégé's gathering in the largest church in Texas, all flying in from every state, each carrying a story of how Florence had instructed and encouraged them in their Christian writing and speaking.... It was not to be. Social media lit up with notes from all over the country, but there would be no love outpouring nor CLASS Reunion for those who had learned from Florence.

After the initial shock and sorrow at the loss of a proper salute to a great lady, I was able to look at a life well lived, and, in an odd way, these memories of a rich and wonderful life both greatly saddened me but also bolstered me to press on, for, no doubt about it, she would have pressed on.

Tuesday, I spent eulogizing Florence. Over twenty years of precious memories I recalled.

Wednesday, I continued making my house perfectly clean. Unnecessary items went to charity. I updated the Master bedroom with a nice basket of silk wildflowers. I might as well add a little decoration too.

In the evening I went to bed early knowing we would be standing in the MRI suite at 7:30 a.m. Prayers continued. Strangely, I slept soundly awaking at the end of this dream:

My girlfriend and I had walked up the winding stairs to the top floor of our high school when on the top step, I felt someone grab my ankle. Alarmed, I tripped, causing my books, pencils and bag to go airborne and making me fall backward into the arms of my tripper, Barry Chatham.

He, looking as though he had no idea what was happening, declared he was glad he had caught me before I fell down all of those stairs below us! Not happy to look down 'all of those stairs,' I was not immediately amused by this prank of an amateur Prince Charming.

We picked up my books, pencils and bag and ran to our U.S. History class just in time for class to start. Once I settled into class, I began to feel a bit differently about the incident as I knew my tripper was a couple of rows behind me also thinking about what had just happened.

That incident, more a remembrance than a dream, was the beginning of seven years of dating, plus 57 years of marriage! What a sweet way to awaken on this last day of my life. On this morning God had given me this remembrance that had been buried under some hard times, some good times, a pandemic and more.

Today was the show down! Once and for all, this vertigo would have a cause and a name; of course, I would have died of a heart attack before the MRI was read, but on we went to the MRI center.

The medical suite was white on white, sterile and chilly. White is good for my 'going home day,' I decided. I asked the technician if my husband, who is in healthcare, could stay in the MRI room during the exam. (Maybe his occupation would make him eligible.) She reluctantly said, 'OK' as she went to the next room to find a chair and the ominous ear plugs. Surely, if he stayed in the room he would intervene if the machine fell and threatened to crush me.

Wanting to get started on the procedure, I went over to the machine to step up and get on the conveyer bed that would take me inside the 'goodbye world' chamber. As I slid inside the tube, I rehearsed my plan of attack.

I would put a smile on my face, do mental exercises releasing tension from feet to head and making me totally relaxed. All of this I did as I prayed for God to help me settle into this 40-minute procedure. No one had told me how long I would be inside the tube, but I had concluded that a big problem would take at least 40 minutes. About that time the technician gave me my last instructions and let me know my MRI would last a total of 20 minutes.

Praise God forever!

Then as God saw it all, the machine wound up for the pounding to start just in time to set the stage for a scene straight from my early life.

Laid out before me, I had a view of the white frame farmhouse of my childhood. At that point, I was viewing it from the west, at the west end of the clothesline.

In an instant, Daddy sauntered around the southeast corner of the house, carrying a step ladder. Whistling as he came, he soon opened the step ladder and climbed near the top. Steadying himself by holding the top of the ladder with one hand, he reached down and pulled the claw hammer from its loop on the side of his overalls. Immediately he began to hammer.

In unison, he hammered in concert with the Star Wars scene inside the MRI. The flashing lights and pounding sound worked well—the pounding to the left, then the right, then up, then down low…then the repeat. Endlessly pounding. The difference for this MRI—the pounding came from my Daddy's hammer. It had been 48 years since I had seen him, and there he was! I have no firm grasp on where I was standing to view all he did, but it appeared that I was a vaporous being, flitting here and there around him as he worked.

Once situated at his work, he reached up to the top of the weather boarding that appeared to have rot on one edge of the board, and with his hammer he clawed the rot away. Then he took a pre-measured and pencil-marked four-inch piece of weather board and slipped this piece into the place he had clawed away. Then he began to hammer it into place. He hammered and hammered until he had it just right.

After about ten minutes the MRI began to readjust. Daddy climbed down and moved his ladder around the corner. With his back to the grapevine and the rhubarb clump, he proceeded to climb up the ladder again to near the top. He did the same clawing of the rotted edges on this side as he had done on the other side. Then he slipped another pre-measured, pencil-marked four-inch piece of weather board into the place he had just cleaned of rot. He got a firm grip on his hammer, and he began to hammer and hammer and hammer until he got the board just like he wanted it.

It was about this time when the MRI technician said, 'We have about five minutes more, and then we're finished, Judy.' With that, I smiled into the Star Wars ceiling of flashing lights and the mirror as I watched Daddy climb back down his ladder, fold it, and carry it along the clothesline. Then he turned, and he was gone.

Grinding and 'carrying on' as it finished its cycle, the MRI machine came to a halt. The sllding converyer slab pushed me out, and I was a new woman!

In summary, I knew then that if God could take a person through an MRI imaging session, as greatly dreaded as mine had been, he can take that person through anything that may come in life until its earthly end. He had given me the devotional written by my friend Jean, given me the remembrance of the strength of one of my teachers, had given me the soothing dream about my boyfriend-become-husband, and topped it off with the most amazing picture of my dear father.

No human that I know could have thought of having my dear Dad be the master of ceremonies of this procedure. No mortal could have pulled me through the MRI event, finally to emerge with joy in my heart. This unforgettable faith-builder showed me that I can do whatever I must do in life because God will never leave me.

Once one lives through such a God-directed experience, she feels driven to tell everyone she meets all about it.

Remember the woman at the well in John 4. She served Jesus of Nazareth a drink of water from the Samaritan well, and she could not wait to tell everyone she met whom she had met and what he had said to her.

A few God-overseen experiences, plus what a friend or acquaintance shares from her own life—that 'something' that only God could do—and the faith-building picks up momentum. When God acts, we stand amazed. This process makes us strong and courageous, just what we long for in times of trouble.

God has said that 'his eyes sweep over the land.' He sees it all unfolding, the good and the evil. On the day when 'the water is rising or the building is burning,' the faith-builder knows God is nearby and is listening for her call to him. He is more than able to steer a clutching one through anything life can toss out into the pathway.

Later in this book when we look at the course of my own faith-building, it is easy to see that in the beginning, it appeared I had little to cling to. I started out with only a poem I learned in high school English Lit class, or a touchstone I learned at camp. At the time, these did seem helpful in consoling me. But then as we move through my life, we see how, quite quickly and with God's help, I built an arsenal of weapons to help me through the trials. I glean truths and strength from time with God. We also see the missed footing, for even the courageous has blips in the system where they forget to draw on the great resource that is theirs. That's when that formerly courageous one becomes the funny lady in the MRI imaging machine. Like Peter, Gospel of Matthew 25, as he stepped out to walk on the water, we must not look away from the One who gives us strength.

God knows what weapons we have in our backpack. He knows what we can withstand and what we cannot. He understands when John 14's 'Let Not Your Heart Be Troubled' is overshadowed by a poem by Robert Louis Stevenson. He meets us where we are. He knows, if we are faithful to follow Him, we are soon to come to discover we have no answers, but he does. When that time comes, we will be strengthened, empowered beyond our own strength. Once we meet him, he saves us presently and he saves us for all time. This change of heart makes us mighty warriors for His Glory.

Coming into a crisis of huge proportions, we may have little patience for listening for God's leading. Resurrection power is spectacular, but it takes time to explain the spectacular. In dire straits, we have little to draw upon. Because some things in life are beyond words to articulate, we, who may be unprepared, must patiently lean in and listen until what pulled Jesus from death unto life is ours to use in our own daily lives. That is living by faith—God-inspired, God-given faith.

BOOT CAMP FOR LIVING ALONG THE PATH WHERE OUR DELIVERER WALKS:

LUKE 7:11-17 NLT

Soon afterward, Jesus went with his disciples to the village of Nain, and a large crowd followed him. A funeral procession was coming out as He approached the city gate. The young man who had died was a widow's only son, and a large crowd from the city was with her. When the Lord saw her, his heart overflowed with compassion.

"Don't cry," he said.

And then he walked over to the coffin and touched it, and the bearers stopped.

"Young man," he said, "I tell you, get up."

Then the dead boy sat up and began to talk!

And Jesus gave him back to his mother.

Great fear swept the crowd, and they praised God, saying, "A mighty prophet has risen among us," and "God has visited his people today."

And the news about Jesus spread throughout Judea and the surrounding countryside.

In faith-building that scene of looking up and seeing Jesus walking toward us in the hour of our greatest sorrow, greatest need, becomes forefront in our faith arsenal.

BOOT CAMP FOR BOILED-DOWN, STRONG, STEADY FAITH:

In a small country church of the 1970s, the minister was a woman. This was in the days when she was the rare lady at every ministerial meeting in the metro area.

She had served in this country church for near 25 years when one day, I approached her with a request. "Please lead a Bible Study on the Book of Revelation. I want to study it, dissect it, and find out what our future holds."

She quietly smiled at my youthful enthusiasm. Then she said words I will never forget. "That's all well and good, but I would like to see you focus on walking with Jesus in everything you do. That will be enough." She encouraged me to get to know him, let him be my friend and constant companion. She wanted me to walk with him and talk with him through every day and every situation.

Unknown to us at the time, It was only a matter of months before calamities began to unfold. All was known by God, of course, but probably not by me in this conversation. But I will draw from her words daily for the rest of my life. Sometimes as the years have passed, I have clung to them in desperation. Rev. Wilma Allen made the Christian life simple, yet complexly powerful. She ended our conversation with stating her favorite song is, "My God and I.'

MY GOD AND I

I B Sergei

(Austris A.Witol)

My God and I go to the field together,
We walk and talk as good friends should and do;
We clasp our hands, our voices ring with laughter—

(You must hear this song online.)
Even though many of us don't know it, everyone goes
through the boot camp of faith-building. To illustrate what
several sets of repetitions looks like, I have included the
'highlights' of my own faith-building years. But first two
principles are in order.

TWO PRINCIPLES TAKEN FROM NATURE SERVE US WELL HERE:

PRINCIPLE # 1. IN FAITH-BUILDING, SCARS DEVELOP FROM WHERE THE PERSON CAME CLOSE TO THE DANGER, AND SURPRISINGLY, FROM WHERE THE PERSON CAME CLOSE TO EVIL SCHEMES TO BLOCK VICTORY.

The following article explains the scarring best. Redwoods and people, have in common the potential for scarring.

USAToday, August 24, 2020

REDWOODS STILL STAND AFTER INFERNO
…"*It was feared that many trees in a grove of old-growth redwoods, some of them 2,000 years old and among the tallest living things on Earth, may finally have succumbed.*

…*The historic park offices are gone as well as are many small buildings and the campground infrastructure as the fire swept through the park about 45 miles south of San Francisco.*

'But the forest is not gone,' said Laura McLindon, conservation director for an environmental group dedicated to the protection of the redwoods and their habitat. 'It will regrow. Every old growth redwood I've ever seen, in Big Basin and other parks, has fire scars on them. They've been through multiple fires, probably worse than this.'"

We survive with God's help, but don't be surprised if there are scars left to commemorate our trial. There may be scarring; there may be a weariness that cannot be put into words, but we will get through with God's help.

Isaiah 43:2 NLT
When you go through the deep waters, I will be with you. When you go through rivers of difficulty, you will not drown. When you walk through the fire of oppression, you will not be burned up, the flames will not consume you.

PRINCIPLE #2. TAKE REST. WHEN GOING THROUGH A TRIAL, DO TAKE REST.

Take rest. A field that has rested gives a bountiful crop---Ovid.

What does a rested field look like?

See this sequence of things the farmer must do, and perhaps we must do, and then see what follows:

Terrace and build up the washed-away banks. Rotate the crops. Restore the nutrients. Kill off the fungus. Look forward to thaw and spring. Cut out the suckers. Likewise, the grapevine stranglers. Go dormant.

Rest.

Divert the floods that wash away rich topsoil. Plant at optimal times. Harvest before the killing frost. Fence the field against varmints. Keep the cows out of the corn. Carry away the rocks. Pick off the beetles.

But most of all, take rest.

Chop out the weeds. Respect the seasons. Prepare for the high water of spring. Check for blight and leaf curl. Understand rust, mold and rot. Discourage the ground hogs.

And, above all, take rest. Give the land a rest.

At Creation, God built rest into every week. That's how important it is for all living things. That includes us. He gave us a Sabbath rest. So important it was to him, he built a day into the week of seven days devoted to rest.

And Jesus said in Matthew 11:28 NLT:

> Come to me, all of you who are weary and carry the heavy burdens, and I will give you rest.

Then with emphasis, he continued in verses 29 and 30:

> Take my yoke upon you. Let me teach you because I am humble and gentle at heart, and you will find rest for your souls. For my yolk is easy to bear, and the burden I give you is light.

With those principles in mind, read the following accounts, the steps that drew me closer to God's power, you can see that my older self drew insight from my younger years as my grandmother played hymns on the piano at church. The repetition of hearing those lyrics over and over again planted what I would need for the remainder of my life.

Those hymns became the umbrella over all of my 'prison and palace' training carrying me through it all.

If my assessment of my own faith-building be true, then it would seem too that you are drawing on what was planted years ago in your own faith-building.

A word of caution is in order. He meets us where we are. We take small, sure steps. Sometimes, but not always, there will be a few leaps and bounds in faith-building, but as the great leaders have used this phrase, most times all we need is enough light to see the next step.

As the Apostle Paul wrote, we work out our faith in 'fear and trembling' and lean into the teachings of God as we make our way.

I.   My father died when I was transitioning between communities and a young mother with a toddler and newborn. To this point, my weapons were pure grit and determination, plus a poem or two. His death at age 55 was a monumental blow. I treasured this short reading and a poem:

NORMAL DAY

…Normal day…
One day I
shall dig my fingers
into the earth, or
bury my face in the
pillow, or stretch my-
self taut, or raise
my hands to the sky,
and want more
than all the world
your return.
--Mary Jean Irion

WHEN SUNDAY LOOKS LIKE TUESDAY

This poem was written by Robert Louis Stevenson

CONSOLATION

…He is not dead…

Push gaily on, strong heart! The while
You travel forward mile by mile,
He loiters with a backward smile
Till you can overtake,
And strains his eyes to search his wake,
Or whistling, as he sees you through the brake,
Waits on a stile.
------------------ Robert Louis Stevenson

My father, only 55 years old, died a few minutes into his night's sleep. His body lay beside my mother, who seeing they had overslept and would miss church services, ran to put on the coffee and then returned to awaken him around 9:00 a.m. the next morning.

He had worked overtime the week before his Saturday night passing. There had been absolutely no warning of his impending death.

The Robert Louis Stevenson poem helped me to believe my father was only a few miles up the road ahead of me. Someday I would see him sitting on a stile waiting for me to join him on our journey together.

II.   Our fourteen-year-old son Stephen was diagnosed with acute lymphatic leukemia six years after the shock of my father's death. A teacher at the local high school, I had been helping my students deal with the leukemia in a fourteen-year-old boy in treatment in a highly respected hospital in Seattle. Far from his hospital, his classmates sent regular messages to cheer him on. In the weeks after our son's diagnosis with the same disease, I could see how my research about my student's illness had provided preparation for my own son's illness. Many steps in Stephen's treatment needed no research, and therefore there was no delay in his treatment because I needed no explanation about that next step. Only two weeks after our son's diagnosis, the student in treatment died. To all of his class, it was a devastating blow to have their friend and then their teacher's son dealing with their well-researched disease.

As I discussed in my book *A Whirlwind's Breath, concerning the events of those days,* every child or adult who had any form of leukemia in those days did not survive for very long. The faces of those people flashed before us as we listened to the diagnosis and protocol for treatment…the two-year-old, the elementary school principal, the music major, my great grandmother and grandfather (yes, very unusual that in 1920 husband and wife died of leukemia and in the same year of Mayo Clinic treatment), and more.

I found help in this trial through journaling with much reflection on family history and trials earlier fathers and mothers had endured. Most of all, I was comforted by resting on this discovery: Jesus loves me. This constant repetition of 'Jesus loves me,' this litany that ran through my thoughts every day seems repetitious and over the top as I write it, but this kind of dialogue with the Savior is what one has when she has nothing. No earthly help comforts in times like these.

JESUS LOVES ME

God has promised he will send the Comforter.

The Comforter tells me:

I am his daughter. My son is his son.

He is preparing a mansion for me, for my son, and he has prepared a way to show us how to find our new home when the time comes to find it.

In the meantime, he has a great plan for me and great plans for my son. He loves us so much he has marked us as his own, and he wants others to see that 'mark' that they too may know him.

All of my days and my son's days are written in his book; he protects us and our whole family. Anyone who harms us, touches the apple of his eye. We are precious in his sight.

He covers me, he covers my son, in protection. He has our backs all day long. Our son's dad and I sign many forms of approval for 100% of his experimental chemotherapy. He oversees each signature. He carries us close to his heart and keeps an eye on us when we wander as though we were toddlers at play. If that's not enough, we have the brush of God on our lives. Angels God has commissioned camp around us as we quickly navigate through the medical protocol for acute disease in this type of leukemia.

Like a loving parent who stands behind the toddler holding both of his hands high above his head as he toddles, God walks with my son through the nights of high body temps, constantly monitoring the drips and spinal taps. He leads our whole family with cords of love and hides us under his wings. Our images are engraved on the palm of his hand.

Furthermore, if we remain attached to him, he will be faithful. Without him, we can do nothing of eternal value. He bends down to feed us Truth and gives us principles for living this life.

He is with us in the watches of the night even when we feel death lurking. He lulls us and he delights in my son with singing in the most dreadful hours when numbers and test results do not sing lulling songs. (When one has been sung to by the Comforter, that person remembers It.) We know that morning will bring his unfailing love, for he heals the broken-hearted, the sick and the weary.

The body we have was perfected at its creation. At the time for a tune-up, The Creator is the one who knows which parts to tweak.

In his love he forgives sin when we call on him to do so. He always greets me with, "Return to me, for I have returned to you." He has hurled our sins into the sea, 'Let the sea deal with it,' I think he must be saying, for he is not going to call my sin back for further observation.

He gave his own son to redeem me, my son.

And now he prunes us, to be the best that we can be. He hems us in as a parent who sets boundaries for a child to live within. To get our attention, he may lay a hand upon the shoulder to steady us, to correct us.

In lovingkindness, he lets us know that everyone who is his child will be corrected when choices are not good for us. Going forward, he leads by the light of his face and his burdens are light. He even helps us to carry them. He will lead all of us into death and take us home to be with him when our earthly life ends.

We can rightfully say, 'He is my friend who walks beside me and sticks closer than a brother or sister. We do life together inside the yoke where he pulls harder than we ever could. He is doing the same for all who call on him.

How great is the love he lavishes on my little family-- and yours too –if you call on him.

After 22 months (in those days) of the most aggressive chemotherapy the oncologist team had approved for his body weight, Stephen's acute lymphatic leukemia was declared in a remission that might hold for five years. After all, he and his fellow teens in the cancer unit with cancers of all kinds were pioneers in survival. Only six years earlier the Doris Lund book, *Eric* assured my high schoolers who read it that there was no cure or promise of remission for acute lymphatic leukemia. At that time no oncologist was declaring a patient had been cured of childhood leukemias or, for that matter, childhood cancers of all types. After the late 70s that was about to change. Praise God.

Two years of Stephen's cancer remission, and I was remembering the five-year pseudo guarantee on that remission. I was sponsoring an active huddle of girls in Fellowship of Christian Athletes. For the annual national retreat, we went to Black Mountain Christian Camp in the Smokey Mountains, near the home of the evangelist Billy Graham.

This was to be a time of athletic retreat for our FCA girls and a rest for me from the day-to-day roller coaster ride of 22 months of chemotherapy for my son.

For the final night of the retreat, a young man from Atlanta had asked if he could speak to 600 girls as this was their last night there. Near the end of his illness, his cancer-riddled body required regularly injected morphine. The leaders of the camp had been advised that he might have to stop mid-speech to have additional pain killer.

I asked God to carry me through this unexpected change to the planned evening. This was a young man my own son's age who was speaking. I had all but lived at Riley Hospital for months and had seen young people near death. I was tough, but this evening was different in that I was a sponsor and didn't have the moment to leave the room and pull myself together. This speech could be almost more than these young people could take in and walk away inspired. We leaders were not certain how to prepare them.

Bruce Banta was escorted to the stage by his team who knew his illness well. I had prayed that God would guide me through what was sure to be a heartbreaking evening.

Amazingly, from the moment Bruce opened his mouth to speak until he was walking away to leave the auditorium, I felt I was encased in an invisible protective bubble. I could hear every word, but the whole evening unfolded like a recollection of another time. As he walked away, the 'bubble' dissolved, and I was again standing with my group from home.

We left the auditorium for our rooms, and I started an all-night Bible Study I will never forget. Not only had God protected me throughout the speech, but he guided me into learning some lessons that he wanted me to know. I felt led to go through the Bible as he pointed out one Scripture after another that answered many questions from the past three years. Never before or since have I had a session like this.

Out of the Scripture he gave me, this passage is the one I could not wait to share with Stephen, now 16 years old. Isaiah 43:17-21...extinguished, snuffed out like a wick; forget the former things, do not dwell on the past. See I am doing a new thing! Now it springs up; do you not perceive it? I am making a way in the desert and streams in the wasteland.

I had no doubt at that time nor since that God had told me the remission from acute lymphatic leukemic would last. I believed it. I knew this was something I could put to rest.

For all who read this I encourage you to seek out all of the many ways God leads you through trying times. For me, this selective Bible 'skip and jump' was just one of many methods he used. He can make things seem like a coincidence, speak through someone else, give your answer through the car radio. He can give you powerful words through someone who doesn't know him or live for him. God can tell us wonderful things by many methods. If there can be any pleasure in the midst of an earth-shattering trial, it is in discovering where God is in all of it.

III.   Our second son Brian, nineteen years old, had back pain and underwent a myelogram which identified the problem with the back, but also uncovered the unthinkable. This procedure awoke a congenital benign brain tumor. In the four months following the myelogram and before further study, Brian had weeks of double vision and unexpected movement of stationary objects. By the time he received his complete diagnosis he had been treated in five hospitals by as many different specialists. Finally, after each specialist sent him on to the next, a neurologist diagnosed the condition as 'an impressively large tumor, developed before his birth, on the right frontal lobe of the brain.'

One evening he described the sensation he felt as the 'floor moving up and slapping him in the face.'

On that evening we were walking near our driveway, but for any help we could give him, we might as well have been fifty miles away. He called the hospital and alerted the ER that he was on his way. When we walked through the door only minutes later, we knew we had walked into an emergency situation.

The following day he had 6-hour ER surgery starting at 2:00 pm, obviously at the end of the regularly scheduled procedures for this neurosurgical team. Even though he had eaten breakfast that day of surgery, the neurosurgeon said his brain stem was unstable, and his body could go into paralysis without immediate relief.

The tumor was shunted, and he began a many-months adjustment to this change. The entire body responded. It seemed as though roll call was awakening each organ, one at a time, to a whole new way of life.

As for the faith-building that came with this unexpected turn of life, there were more previous times of leaning on God from which to draw strength. We had been through life-threatening illness in a child. However, this time, there was a feeling of 'this was not fair' added to the diagnosis and treatment. Somehow, we mortals believe that once we have served, we don't have to serve again!

With Stephen we soon saw that other people were suffering. Why should we feel our family was exempt from childhood cancers-- 'Into every life some rain must fall.' Unknown to us, we had made a mental note to ourselves saying, 'Thankfully we have served our time with the trials of life.' While other people were building houses, going on extended family vacations, we had been leaning on hospital walls waiting for any bit of good news that could be dispensed. Now that we had served and were now so richly blessed-- our first son had a future-- we could 'fold our tent on oncology' or really any other threat to human life. Childhood leukemia had been a huge blow, not a small misstep.

After our initial response with the second diagnosis, we realized the problem remained. Our second son was seriously ill, and the illness was in the same category as that of his older brother-life threatening.

Does a family get two blessings of the same magnitude? It was possible that God was not going to bless us with yet another child's restored health.

Those thoughts were undeniably there, but I could not deny that God was hovering over us on the day of the diagnosis and through the recovery from the surgery.

On that day of diagnosis, the neurosurgeon had entered the room in a nonchalant way, was unusually personable and chatty with Brian. It was a Tuesday-kind-of-ordinary day. Then he had to deliver the diagnosis to Brian and his mother. And he did.

Brian's dad and I knew how to keep work and home going smoothly. Yesterday he had been with Brian during the day; today I was there. My presence was most fortunate now that I have time to look back and be grateful, for if I had not heard that conversation, I would have always questioned or wanted more facts. This way I knew exactly what the neurosurgeon had seen, his view of the prognosis and recovery. He ended his diagnosis with "Brian we will have you up and playing ball in no time."

A nineteen-year-old has a different view of things than a fourteen-year- old has. He needed space and time to think about what he had just heard. From much earlier coaching, I knew that was coming, plus I needed to go somewhere so I could fall apart without his seeing me do so.

I quietly left him after he told me he just wanted to be alone. Once outside, I ran through a light rain to my car which I had parked in a far-removed lot. Windshield wipers on and car temperature adjusted, I settled in to process what I had just heard. Overlooked by me, the radio had come on as I adjusted the car temperature. Immediately---within twenty minutes of the diagnosis—the David Meece song 'Wonderfully Made' gave God's message to me. The song is based upon Psalm 139:14-16 NIV

I praise you because I am fearfully and wonderfully made, your works are wonderful, I know that full well. My frame was not hidden from you when I was made in the secret place. When I was woven together in the depths of the earth, your eyes saw my unformed body. All the days ordained for me were written in your book before one of them came to be.

For the moment that song spoke wonderful truth to me, but then two predictable questions emerged. What caused the tumor to form during the pregnancy of nineteen years ago? Did God know and not somehow warn us as he played in baseball and football games and in other childhood activities?

Again, after all of the speculating about whatever caused this and whether God knew, after all of that, everything I needed to know was answered in Psalm 139:14-16.

(Another significant comfort came to me on the night of the surgery as I sat beside a window only a few feet from the hospital's lifeline helicopter pad. Awaiting the expected seizures Brian would experience, I remembered the lines of 'Away In A Manger.' that matched our situation in 'Bless all the dear children in Thy tender care...' I will discuss this in more detail later in the book.)

IV. To this point I have discussed three huge trials: my father's death, Stephen's leukemia, and Brian's brain tumor. The fourth trial, everyone probably has in some version, therefore, I wanted to include it here in our faith-building. In some form all of us have a dread and fear of something we have seen repeatedly occur in our family. Examples of such:

a. Every 'bad thing' that has happened in our extended family has occurred in November. Beware of November.

b. Every health crisis in our family has occurred in January. New diagnoses. You name it, we've had it.

c. My two sisters and my mother died at age 78. This year I turn 78. Now what?

I have my own albatross-item. We will include it here as faith-builder # 4:

One of the most feared cancers in the United States, if not in the world today, is pancreatic cancer. When my family started 'dealing with it,' the prognosis was three months of life after diagnosis, but for some death could come within weeks.

My paternal grandfather's death certificate stated he died of pancreatic cancer, but it had been an outgrowth of uncontrolled diabetes; therefore, we children thought he had died of Diabetes II.

Our 91-year-old grandmother's illness lasted three weeks. Three weeks before her death, she attended a wedding anniversary celebration and happily stood beside her grandson for a photograph. By the time of her passing, we who loved her dearly, were thinking she had suffered for a very long time.

Next her daughter, my aunt, lived with pancreatic cancer for four months. Her diagnosis came shortly after she had turned down an ice cream treat on a family outing as she stated 'food just doesn't taste that good lately.' All of her life, she had purposely planned her meals to include the fresh garden produce, fruit from the local orchard and had always been active. Because of her efforts to keep healthy, the doctor said she would probably live four months whereas others would live three. She chose not to have chemotherapy or hospitalization.

Next, my mother was diagnosed with pancreatic cancer so early that the oncologist said she didn't have it on this day, but she would have it very soon.

The growth had not started causing the symptoms. She lived 18 months. By the time of her illness, the prognosis for patients with pancreatic cancer had risen to 9% survival for five years.

A year later, on the paternal side of our family, my first cousin was diagnosed with pancreatic cancer. He lived only weeks.

Only recently the sixth person in my family tree died of pancreatic cancer—a third cousin.

While some in my family had lived very carefully, worked the land around them, ate the garden produce and found themselves in a church pew every Sunday, that didn't seem to make much difference in their round with this dreaded disease. I heard a doctor say, "It doesn't matter what one tries. There are no preventative measures for this one."

So you see, everyone has a version of what I have just described—that albatross around the neck as in the Samuel Coleridge poem 'The Rime of the Ancient Mariner.'

How does this figure into the faith-building plan?

I keep the Bible Verse handy---We live by faith, not by sight. II Corinthians 5:7

These words include not living by percentages of survival rates. We don't live by experiences of people in our community or by experiences of people in our families. As I learned in trial #3, we are fearfully made and our days are in God's hands. We are not our brother nor our sister, We, individually live out our days.

So, you see, these two verses, in faith, lead me though trail #4: II Corinthians 5:7 and Psalm 139:14

V. Unlike the trials before, this one had a different tone to it. Perhaps others have had similar experiences. We've had polio, typhoid fever, smallpox, Spanish flu epidemics in the past. In 2020 we had a pandemic of the coronavirus COVID 19. Perhaps the faith-builders who read this had a parent or cousin who had polio during the 1950s or typhoid fever in 1933 or so. You will identify.

My trial #5 includes another component to the disease. ER personnel, First Responders, and people in the military will identify with this faith- builder.

In April and May of 2020 our granddaughter, a trained ER nurse, was deployed with the Naval Corps of Nurses to serve in the Jacob Javits field hospital in New York City to care for the overflow of patients suffering with COVID 19. Every day the new reports were more devastating. The virus, killing thousands all over the world, had settled with a vengeance in New York City.

On March 29, 2020, she knew she had her assignment.

April 5,2020, Sunday, 8:47 a.m.
Indianapolis, Indiana

Love you Guys!
Such a whirlwind I'm about to throw my phone away so tired of it ringing…leaving for New Jersey tonight, then to New York City tomorrow. I believe that is the plan. I will be working at the Jacob Javits Center and stay in a hotel nearby….
Brittany

April 6, 2020, Monday

Indiana

Brittany, I heard Lady A (formerly Lady Antebellum) singing, 'What I'm Leaving For." I am sending it to you because you know your contemporary music and the poignant words to these lyrics agree with your thoughts as you are leaving.

Got my bags packed, got my ticket
Got a headache to go with it….

April 7, 2020, Tuesday

From Indiana to New York City

The eyes of the Lord search the whole earth in order to strength those whose hearts are fully committed to him…. II Chronicles 16:9

Brittany---
Since my Grandmother Lois was the piano player of the county, I learned to know the words of the hymns of the church very early. So each day you are deployed, I will

give you a line or two of those same songs in order to encourage you too. I will try to send them at the end of your shift each evening.

Here's the first one—Enjoy!

THIS IS MY FATHER'S WORLD
Maltbie D. Babcock, 1901 Franklin L. Sheppard

This is my Father's world,
He shines in all that's fair,
In the rustling grass
I hear him pass,
He speaks to me everywhere.

In the rusting grass, I hear him pass,
He speaks to me everywhere.

(Powerful image: God walking in the rustling grass...I hear him pass...)

NOTE TO READER:

April 6, 2020 New York City has had 3,200 deaths from this virus. By comparison, on September 11, 2001, New York City had 2,753 deaths. Remember how our hearts were shattered upon hearing this 9/11 news?

April 6, 2020, *The Indianapolis Star*
A nurse pleaded, "Please take this seriously. People are dying. I am witnessing it. This is not the media blowing it out of proportion. It's not a political stunt. It's happening. It's here and it's real."

April 8, 2020, Wednesday
Indiana to New York City

'Blessed Assurance' is a hymn I remember hearing my dad sing. He was standing behind me each Sunday while in church; therefore, I could hear him well. Of course, Grandmother was playing the piano. She didn't have a soft touch—she practically stood as she struck each note.

BLESSED ASSURANCE

Fanny J. Crosby Mrs. J. F. Knapp

This is my story,
This is my song...

...Waiting and watching,
Looking above,
Filled with his goodness,
Lost in his love.

New York City is holy ground right now...people transitioning from here to life beyond. Living, dying, watching, waiting... the whole country is watching and waiting.

My dad----your great grandpa
My grandmother---your great, great grandmother

April 9, 2020, Thursday

Indiana to New York City

In Grandmother's church, today would be called Maundy Thursday: The Last Supper Remembrance for Christians.

Grandmother was a whiz at playing rallying songs. As I said she struck the keys of the piano quite deliberately.

ONWARD CHRISTIAN SOLDIERS

Sabine Baring-Gould Arthur Sullivan

Onward Christian Soldiers,
Marching as to war,
With the cross of Jesus
Going on before!

She played this for the start of the children's penny marches when they were instructed to put their money in the basket designated for missions. Down the aisle we went bouncing to the music and dropping our money into the basket.

(We will learn that today was one of the deadliest days in Indiana and other locations for the virus' death toll.)

April 10, 2020, Good Friday

Indiana to New York City

BENEATH THE CROSS OF JESUS

Elizabeth C. Clephane Frederick C. Maker

Vs. 3

I take, O cross, thy shadow

For my abiding place;

I ask no other sunshine

Than the sunshine of His face;

Content to let the world go by,

To know no gain or loss,

My sinful self my only shame,

My glory all the cross.

(I can hear Grandmother playing this one right now. It has good alto in it.)

April 11, 2020, Saturday

The day between Good Friday and Easter Sunday

IN THE GARDEN

C.A.M. C. Austin Miles

I come to the garden alone,
While the dew is still on the roses…

(A beautiful song---listen to it online and be renewed!)

April 12, 2020, Easter Sunday
Indiana to New York City
(We are celebrating Easter Sunday online today. All in Indiana are in quarantine.)

My favorite Easter song…well, Grandmother got a bit dramatic on this one. She teased it a bit with a very soft beginning, and then came to the 'He arose' with a loud sound, like in your childhood when a jack-in-the-box jumped out. Certainly, this song, this Easter song speaks to me, has deep meaning, but I smile when I say it, I did love the way she played it.

CHRIST AROSE
Robert Lowry Robert Lowry

Low in the grave He lay—
Jesus, my Savior!
Waiting the coming day—
Jesus, my Lord!

(Then she picked up the tempo.)

Up from the grave He arose,

With a mighty triumph o'er His foes;

He arose a Victor from the dark domain,

And He lives forever with His saints to reign.

(LOUD)

He arose!

He arose!

Hallelujah! Christ arose!

(Also, today, I didn't get to hear the drummer in our church orchestra beat out the dirge-like rhythm behind our singing of 'When I Survey the Wondrous Cross.'

WHEN I SURVEY THE WONDROUS CROSS

Isaac Watts Lowell Mason

Vs. 3,4

See, from His head, His hands, His feet,

Sorrow and love flow mingled down;

Did e'er such love and sorrow meet,

Or thorns compose so rich a crown?

Were the whole realm of nature mine,

That were a present far too small;

Love so amazing, so divine,

Demands my soul, my life, my all.

(Wonderful word picture. I wish I had written that!)

April 13, 2020, Monday
Indiana to New York City

My next favorite Easter song I will send you today on this Easter Monday. This one has a funny story to go with it. Sister Karen is four years younger than I. As Grandmother had all of us whipped up and singling loudly, Karen, who was probably six years old to my older and wiser 10 years old, really 'got into' the song in verse 3:

HE LIVES

A.H.Ackley A. H. Ackley

Rejoice, Rejoice, O Christian,
Lift up your jaws and sing...

(What? Lift up your jaws and sing? How embarrassing!
I hope no one heard that.)

(You will want to listen to this one online.)

April 14, 2020, Tuesday
Indiana to New York City

This hymn fits your nursing duties these days.

RESCUE THE PERISHING

Fanny J. Crosby William H. Doane

Rescue the perishing,
Care for the dying;
Jesus is merciful,
Jesus will save.

Rescue the perishing,
Duty demands it;
Strength for my labor
The Lord will provide.

April 15, 2020, Wednesday

Indiana to New York City

Song for today:

Grandmother had the piano jumping on this one.

GLORY TO HIS NAME

E. A. Hoffman J. H. Stockton

Down at the cross where my Savior died,
Down where for cleansing from sin I cried,
There to my heart was the blood applied;
Glory to His name.

Glory to His name,
Glory to His name;
There to my heart was the blood applied;
Glory to His name.

April 16, 2020, Thursday

Indiana to New York City

GIVE OF YOUR BEST TO THE MASTER

H. R. G. Charlotte A. Barnard

Give of your best to the Master,
Give of the strength of your youth;
Throw your soul's fresh, glowing ardor
Into the battle for truth.

Jesus has set the example—
Dauntless was He, young and brave;
Give Him your loyal devotion,
Give Him the best that you have.

Give of your best to the Master,
Give of the strength of your youth;
Clad in salvation's full armour,
Join in the battle for truth.

Your grandpa had two brothers, Lee and Larry. When he was 15, and Lee was 16, Lee died of complications of the seasonal flu. Infection settled in the brain resulting in spinal meningitis. This song, 'Give of Your Best to the Master,' was played at his funeral.

Over 50 years later, school mates said it made a great impression on their lives. Lee was a jolly fellow. He played the bass drum in the school band in which he would have played the evening he died.

We had a special dance program made up for the band show that ran that night. Our dance music was set to the popular 'Fascination,' a song of that time.

FASCINATION

Chorus:
It was fascination, I know…

(I can even remember a couple of the dance steps! All of this on a night just before the news came that none of us will ever forget. Lee is your great uncle.)

April 17, 2020, Friday
Indiana to New York City

Grandmother played this song. Decades later I used a phrase from it as the title for my earlier book, *A Whirlwind's Breath*.

FAITH IS THE VICTORY
John G. Yates Ira D. Sankey

Vs. 2

His banner over us is love,

Our sword the Word of God:

We tread the road the saints above

With shouts of triumph trod,

By faith, they like a whirlwind's breath,

Swept on o'er every field;

The faith by which they conquered death

Is still my shining shield.

Faith is the Victory!

Faith is the Victory!

O glorious Victory,

That overcomes the world.

We draw strength from the saints who have gone before us. I have one grandmother whose 21-year- old son died of undiagnosed and untreated infantile paralysis (polio). She had nine more children. Any mother could imagine that she wondered if they, too, would die of this mysterious disease.

I have another grandmother (the piano player of this discussion) whose young husband died in 1927 partly because we did not yet have antibiotics. He had an appendectomy followed by infection. This grandmother had four daughters, ages 2,4, 10, 14, and the whole country fell into the Great Depression two years after his death. She fed her children off the land, foraging for wild blackberries and using popcorn for cereal.

Our forefathers and foremothers teach us much about living through trying times.

April 18, 2020, Saturday
Indiana to New York City

Ora Mae, mother of ten children and paternal grandmother to me, also played the piano. She played on a piano that was never professionally tuned, in my years at home anyway, and her four youngest children often sang this song with her as she played:

UNDER HIS WINGS
William O. Cushing Ira D. Sankey

Under His wings
I am safely abiding;
Though the night deepens
And tempests are wild,
Still I can trust Him;
I know He will keep me;
He has redeemed me,
And I am His child.

Under His wings,
Under His wings,
Who from His love can sever?
Under His wings
My soul shall abide,
Safely abide forever.

April 18, 2020, Sunday
Indiana to New York City

(This song is associated with one of your favorite verses--
Isaiah 6:8 'Here am I, send me!'

TAKE MY LIFE AND LET IT BE
Frances R. Havergal C.H.A. MaLan

Take my life, and let it be
Consecrated, Lord, to Thee;
Take my hands, and let them move
At the impulse of Thy love,
At the impulse of Thy love.

Take my feet, and let them be
Swift and beautiful for Thee;
Take my voice, and let me sing,
Always, only for my King,
Always, only for my King.
> (Beautiful line—'Take my hands and let them move at the impulse of Thy love.')

April 19, 2020, Monday
Indiana to New York City

This song Grandmother often played at funerals. The words speak to us these days.

ABIDE WITH ME
H. F. LYTLE W. H. Mone

Abide with me;
Fast falls the eventide;
The darkness deepens;
Lord, with me abide.
When other helpers fail,
And comforts flee,
Help of the helpless,
O abide with me!

April 20, 2020, Tuesday
Indiana to New York City

'Teach me some melodious sonnet,
Sung by flaming tongues above'

COME THOU FOUNT
Robert Robinson John Wyeth

Come, thou fount of every blessing,
Tune my heart to sing Thy grace;

Streams of mercy, never ceasing,

Call for songs of loudest praise.

Teach me some melodious sonnet,

Sung by flaming tongues above;

Praise the mount—I'm fixed upon it—

Mount of Thy redeeming love.

O to Grace how great a debtor

Daily I'm constrained to be!

Let Thy goodness, like a fetter,

Bind my wandering heart to Thee;

Prone to wander, Lord, I feel it,

Prone to leave the God I love;

Here's my heart, O take and seal it;

Seal it for Thy courts above.

April 21, 2020, Wednesday
Indiana to New York City

THERE IS A FOUNTAIN
William Cowper Lowell Mason

Vs.4

E'er since by faith I saw the stream
Thy flowing wounds supply,
Redeeming love has been my theme,
And shall be till I die;
And shall be till I die,
Redeeming love has been my theme,
And shall be till I die.

April 22, 2020, Thursday
Indiana to New York City

The old piano had to be nailed down when Grandmother Lois Stackhouse Ham Leonard played this one---

VICTORY IN JESUS

E.M.B. E. M. Bartlett

I heard an old, old story,
How a Savior came from glory....

(See the words to this one online. It is loaded with encouragement.)

April 23, 2020, Friday
Indiana to New York City

AWAY IN A MANGER
M.L. Martin Luther

Vs. 3
Be near me, Lord Jesus,
I ask You to stay
Close by me forever,
And love me, I pray;
Bless all the dear children
In Thy tender care,
And take us to heaven,
To live with Thee there.

On the day of Brian's surgery for the brain tumor, I spent the night in a chair in his room in the Children's Wing of Methodist Hospital in Indianapolis. His room was on the same level as the pad for the hospital's AirEvac Lifeteam, and the view from his window was the coming and going of the helicopter.

I had been told to expect Brian to have seizures in the hours after his surgery; however, he never moved. I heard only groans. Groans from deep down where no one else felt the invasive hurt.

His roommate, a nine-year-old whose name and story we did not know, proudly wore his new tennis shoes to bed- -laced up and tied. They were the sought-after Michael Jordan basketball shoes, a get-well gift from his family.

Visiting hours over, the hospital quiet, yet a potential crisis was simmering; every nurse visit to monitor the various machines surrounding Brian's bed could change the situation quickly. Most of the night the room was dark with the only light coming from the monitors and the window where I was looking out at the twitching lights of the helicopter pad. The scene outside and the scene inside, both poised for an emergency of life and death proportions.

In times like these, the one who stands by pulls from what she already knows. This setting had no television programs blaring, afforded no book reading, for even the turn of a page could rouse the sleeper and his roommate, both needing the rest. I silently repeated the above verse 3 of "Away in a Manger."

I want to give you that verse again:

Be near me, Lord Jesus,
I ask Thee to stay
Close by me forever,
And love me, I pray;
Bless all the dear children
In Thy tender care,
And take us to heaven,
To live with Thee there.

April 24, 2020, Saturday
Indiana to New York City

LET THE LOWER LIGHTS BE BURNING
P.P. Bliss P.P. Bliss

Trim your feeble lamp, my brother;
Some poor sailor tempest tossed,
Trying now to make the harbor,
In the darkness maybe lost.

Let the lower lights be burning!
Send a beam across the wave!
Some poor fainting struggling seaman

You may rescue,

You may save.

(Symbols: Lower lights, down at ground level, those lights that twitch and turn below the lighthouse lamp. Then there is the one upper light, the light from the lighthouse tower. In the Christian world the Lighthouse symbolizes God, and we are the lower lights who work to glorify God as we minister to others in time of need.)

April 26, 2020, Sunday
Indiana to New York City

As a young girl, I wanted to be the basketball queen at my high school. Doesn't every girl have a similar dream? Therefore, the following song speaks to me, on the human level, of course. Hope it does to you too!

WILL THERE BE ANY STARS IN MY CROWN
Eliza E. Hewitt John R. Sweeney

Oh, what joy it will be when His face I behold,
Living gems at His feet to lay down;

It would sweeten my bliss in the city of gold,
Should there be any stars in my crown.

Will there be any stars,
Any stars in my crown
When at evening the sun goeth down?
When I wake with the blessed
In the mansions of rest,
Will there be any stars in my crown?

April 27, 2020, Monday
Indiana to New York City

Be blest with this one!

TURN YOUR EYES UPON JESUS
H.H.L. Helen Howard Lemmel

Turn your eyes upon Jesus,
Look full in His wonderful face....

(Hear this one online. Two of the older women of the
church loved this one and in turn, I learned the words
and love it too.)

April 28, 2020, Tuesday
Indiana to New York City

WHISPERING HOPE
A.H. Alice Hawthorne

Soft as the voice of an angel,
Breathing a lesson unheard,
Hope with a gentle persuasion
Whispers her comforting word;
Wait 'til the darkness is over,
Wait 'til the tempest is done,
Hope for the sunshine tomorrow,
After the shower is gone.

Whispering hope,
O welcome thy voice,
Making my heart
In its sorrow rejoice.

April 29, 2020, Wednesday
Indiana to New York City

(Hear this one sung by a person with a deep, rich Elvis-type voice)

NO NOT ONE
Johnson Oatman, Jr. George C. Hugg

There's not an hour that He's not near (me,)
No not one! No not one!
No night so dark, but His love can cheer (me,)
No not one! No not one!

Jesus knows all about our struggles,
He will guide 'til the day is done;
There's not a friend like the lowly Jesus,
No not one! No not one!

April 30, 2020, Thursday
Indiana to New York City

SWING LOW
African Spiritual

Swing low, Sweet chariot,

Comin' for to carry me home;

Swing low, Sweet chariot,

Comin' for to carry me home.

I looked over Jordan

And what did I see?

Comin' for to carry me home;

A band of angels comin' after me,

Comin' for to carry me home.

Swing low, Sweet chariot,

Comin' for to carry me home;

Swing low, Sweet chariot,

Comin' for to carry me home.

(I used this title for a book—'Swing Low.')

May 1, 2020, Friday

Indiana to New York City

Brittany, I sent you the song that I associate with Brian's illness; now I will send you the song that I associate with your dad's leukemia illness. I sang it over and over---in my mind, of course! You hear it often in churches today.

GREAT IS THY FAITHFULNESS
T.O. Chisholm William M. Runyon

Vs.2,

'Summer and winter,
Springtime and harvest
Sun, moon and stars
In their courses above....'

(Do see the words to this song online!)

May 2, 2020, Saturday
Indiana to New York City

Grandmother liked to play the following hymn. No doubt that is where my mother first heard it, for Mother liked to sing this song in her I-am-on-Broadway voice as she worked in the kitchen.)

HEAVENLY SUNLIGHT
Rev. H. J. Zelley G.H.Cook

Walking in sunlight, all of my journey;
Over the mountains, thro-the deep vale;
Jesus has said, "I'll never forsake thee,"
Promise divine that never can fail.

Heavenly sunlight,
Heavenly sunlight,
Flooding my soul with glory divine:
Hallelujah, I am rejoicing,
Singing His praises,
Jesus is mine.

May 3, 2020, Sunday
Indiana to New York City

As a writer, I love vs. 3:

THE LOVE OF GOD
F.M.L. F. M. Lehman

This song you can find online is one you will enjoy, especially the lines regarding writing.

O, love of God
How rich and pure!
How measureless and strong!...

May 4, 2020, Monday
Indiana to New York City

MY TRIBUTE
Andre Crouch

If you are looking for a treat pull this up on your smart phone. I peck it out on my piano almost every day.

'How can I say thanks
For the things you have done for me?
Things so undeserved...'

May 5, 2020, Tuesday

Indiana to New York City

I once saw Gloria Gaither pull out the paper on which she had written the words to 'Because He Lives.' If she and Bill Gaither had never written another song, this one would have been enough.

BECAUSE HE LIVES
Gloria Gaither William Gaither

God sent his Son,
They called him Jesus,
He came to love, heal and forgive;
He bled and died
To buy my pardon,
An empty grave is there
To prove my Savior lives.

Chorus:

Because He lives I can face tomorrow
Because He lives all fear is gone
Because I know He holds the future
And life is worth the living
Just because He lives.

May 6, 2020, Wednesday

Indiana to New York City

I'VE JUST SEEN JESUS

Gloria Gaither, William J. Gaither, Danny Daniels

I've just seen Jesus!
I tell you He's alive!
I've just seen Jesus,
My precious Lord, alive.
And I know
He really saw me too;
As if 'til now
I'd never lived.
All that I've done before
Won't matter anymore.
I've just seen Jesus,
And I'll never be the same again.

May 7, 2020, Thursday
Indiana to New York City

HE TOUCHED ME
William J. Gaither William J. Gaither

Shackled by a heavy burden,
'Neath a load of guilt and shame—
Then the hand of Jesus touched me,
And now I am no longer the same.

He touched me! O, He touched me!
And O the joy that floods my soul!
Something happened, and now I know,
He touched me and made me whole.

May 8, 2020, Friday
Indiana to New York City

The following song was a favorite of a quartet in which
your great, grandfather sang bass:

IN TIMES LIKE THESE
R. C. J. Ruth Caye Jones

You will want to find this on You Tube. It was an important part of my young life as I was making decisions that I knew would chart my future.

May 9, 2020, Saturday
Indiana to New York City

Before the husband of my friend passed away, I wrote the lyrics to this song and sent it to him. His nurse recalled the hymn from her own past, and when she got him ready for the day, she sang this song as she worked. I was so honored that she, my friend and her husband were blessed by the recall of this old hymn, which is a happy, rich song.

I WILL SING THE WONDROUS STORY
Frances Rowley Peter Philip Bilhorn

Vs. 2,3

I was lost when Jesus found me,
Found the sheep that went astray,
Threw His loving arms around me,
Drew me back into His way.

Yes, I'll sing the wondrous story
Of the Christ who died for me,
Sing it with the saints in glory
Gathered by the crystal sea.

I was bruised but Jesus healed me'
Faint was I from many a fall;
Sight was gone, and fears possessed me,
But He freed me from them all.

Yes, I'll sing the wondrous story
Of the Christ who died for me
Sing it with the saints in glory
Gathered by the crystal sea.

May 10, 2020, Sunday

Indiana to New York City

MORNING HAS BROKEN

'Morning Has Broken' is a song for the mornings of summertime. Also, it is a description of that first morning after Creation. Be blest by looking for it on your i-phone. It was written by Eleanor Farjeon and Yusuf Islam.

May 11, 2020, Monday
Indiana to New York City

HIGHER GROUND
Johnson Oatman, Jr. Charles H. Gabriel

Vs. 2

My heart has no desire to stay
Where doubts arise and fears dismay;
Tho' some may dwell where these abound,
My prayer, my aim is higher ground.

Lord, lift me up and let me stand
By faith on Heaven's tableland,
A higher plane than I have found;
Lord, plant my feet on higher ground.

May 12,2020, Tuesday

Indiana to New York City

So, what did you just do for love? Looks like you are doing a lot in your work in the field hospital during the pandemic.

When I was teaching and your dad had just come out of his chemotherapy for leukemia, my school did a fundraiser for research for childhood cancers. It was a talent show, with their own talent and the theme song was "What I Did For Love."

Today I will send you two songs—a hymn and that theme song.

SEND THE LIGHT

C. H. G. CHARLES H. GABRIEL

There's a call comes ringing

O'er the restless wave,

Send the light! Send the light!

There are souls to rescue,

There are souls to save,

Send the light!

Send the light!

Let us not grow weary
In the work of love,
Send the light! Send the light!
Let us gather jewels
For a crown above,
Send the light! Send the light!

Send the light,
The blessed gospel light;
Let it shine from shore to shore!
Send the light!
The blessed gospel light!
Let it shine forevermore.

Online--
Check out the words for 'What I Did For Love'-- a beautiful
show tune by Marvin Hamlisch

May 13, 2020, Wednesday
Indiana to New York City

I AM THINE, O LORD
Fanny Crosby W. H. Doane

Vs. 1 and 3

I am Thine, O Lord,
I have heard Thy voice,
And it told Thy love to me;
But I long to rise in the arms of faith,
And be closer drawn to Thee.

Draw me nearer, nearer,
Blessed Lord,
To the cross where Thou hast died;
Draw me nearer, nearer, nearer,
Blessed Lord,
To Thy precious bleeding side.

O the pure delight of a single hour
That before Thy throne I spend,
When I kneel in prayer,
And with Thee, my God,
I commune as friend with friend!

(I once heard an elderly lady say, "You will probably be alone or uncomfortable when God speaks to you most clearly." I imagine you feel that in your present quarantine.)

May 14, 2020, Thursday

Indiana to Portsmouth, Virginia quarantine

Grandmother played this song as a round. When she came to the chorus, a few altos joined the sopranos and then all of us came together at the end of the song.

STILL SWEETER EVERY DAY

W. C. MARTIN C. AUSTIN MILES

To Jesus every day I find my heart is closer drawn;
He's fairer than the glory of the old and purple dawn;
He's all my fancy pictures in its fairest dreams, and more;
Each day He grows still sweeter than He was the day before.

Chorus: The half has not been fancied
This side the golden shore;
O, there He'll be still sweeter than He was the day before.

(Meanwhile, the altos were singing, picking up the tempo along with us)

The half cannot be fancied
This side the golden shore;
(The half cannot be fancied

This side the golden shore;)
O there He'll be still sweeter
Than He was the day before.
(O there He'll be still sweeter
Than He was the day before.)

May 15, 2020, Friday

Indiana to Portsmouth, Virginia in quarantine

WE GATHER TOGETHER
FOLK SONG OF THE NETHERLANDS

Beside us to guide us,
Our God with us joining,
Ordaining, maintaining
His Kingdom divine;
So from the beginning
The fight we are winning,
Thou, Lord, wast at our side—
The glory be Thine!

May 16, 2020, Saturday

Indiana to Portsmouth, Virginia in quarantine

Lots of thoughts on your mind now in your fourth day of quarantine. "Farther Along" would be a great hymn to check out on your i-phone. The lyrics are good for sorting things out.

Farther along
We'll know all about it,
Farther along, we'll understand why...

May 17, 2020, Sunday

Indiana to Portsmouth, Virginia in 5th day quarantine

When I was sixteen years old, this was my favorite song, and therefore remains special to me. When I hear the piano strike the first notes, I know what's coming!

FAIREST LORD JESUS
Anonymous Arr. R. S. Willis

Fairest Lord Jesus,
Ruler of all nature,

O Thou of God and man the Son,

Thee will I cherish,

Thee will I honor,

Thou my soul's glory, joy, and crown.

Fair are the meadows,

Fairer still the woodlands,

Robed in the blooming garb of spring;

Jesus is fairer,

Jesus is purer,

Who makes the woeful heart to sing.

Fair is the sunshine,

Fairer still the moonlight,

And all the twinkling, starry host;

Jesus shines brighter,

Jesus shines purer,

Than all the angels heaven can boast.

May 18, 2020, Monday

Indiana to Portsmouth, Virginia in sixth day of quarantine

(This is the way we talk with Jesus:)

WHITER THAN SNOW
JAMES NICHOLSON WILLIAM G. FISCHER

VS. 3,4

Lord Jesus, for this I most humbly entreat,
I wait, blessed Lord, at Thy crucified feet;
By faith, for my cleansing,
I see Thy blood flow—
Now wash me,
And I shall be whiter than snow.

Lord Jesus, Thou seeest I patiently wait,
Come now, and within me
A new heart create;
To those who have sought Thee,
Thou never said no—
Now wash me
And I shall be whiter than snow.

Whiter than snow,
Yes, whiter than snow;
Now wash me,
And I shall be
Whiter than snow.

May 19, 2020, Tuesday

Indiana to Portsmouth, Virginia in seventh day of quarantine

(I often send this one as a sympathy card.)

DOES JESUS CARE?
Frank E. Graeff J. Lincoln Hall

Vs. 2
Does Jesus care when my way is dark
With a nameless dread and fear?
As the daylight fades into deep nightshades,
Does He care enough to be near?

O, Yes, He cares,
I know He cares,
His heart is touched by my grief;
When the days are weary,
The long nights dreary,
I know my Savior cares.

May 20, 2020, Wednesday

Indiana to Portsmouth, Virginia in eighth day of quarantine

GOD BE WITH YOU

J. E. Rankin W. G. Tomer

Vs. 1,2,4

God be with you 'til we meet again,

By His counsels guide, uphold you,

With His sheep securely fold you;

God be with you 'til we meet again.

God be with you 'til we meet again,

'Neath His wings protecting hide you,

Daily manna will provide you;

God be with you 'til we meet again.

God be with you 'til we meet again;

Keep love's banner floating o'er you,

Smited death's threatening wave before you;

God be with you 'til we meet again.

(In the field hospital you could identify with verse 4)

May 21, 2020, Thursday

Indiana to Portsmouth, Virginia, in ninth day of quarantine

I am including this story as told to me, where it originated, I do not know:

In 1932 when the United States was as poor as it could be, a young musician and his wife lived in Chicago waiting for his big break in the music world. His wife was due to have their first child when he was called to go to St. Louis to perform. He had to go.

The following evening as he was performing in the intense St. Louis heat, he received a telegram mid-show when the performance was going well. The telegram had a short message: 'Your wife just died.'

She had given birth to a boy who shortly after her death died also.

After her and their son's funeral, he went with his friend to a local music school on the Southside of Chicago. The story goes that it was very quiet there. The night was late when he sat down at the piano and played odds and ends of songs. The music soothed him as he played. And---in a short time he had completely composed the following song:

TAKE MY HAND, PRECIOUS LORD

You will find the lyrics on your i-phone.

(This young musician was later to be known as the great Big Band era's Tommy Dorsey who for years accompanied singer Frank Sinatra and other singers.)

May 22, 2020, Friday

Indiana to

Portsmouth, Virginia in tenth day of quarantine

PUT YOUR HAND IN THE HAND

Gene MacLellan Sony has the copyright

You will want to find this song on your i-phone, also; it is very comforting.

'Put your hand in the hand of the man from Galilee...'

May 23, 2020, Saturday

Indiana to Portsmouth, Virginia eleventh day of quarantine

Here's one that really helped me through some hard days—'A Thing Called Love'
Written by Jerry Reed and recorded by several, including Elvis Presley. Hear his recording of it on your i-phone.

May 24, 2020, Sunday

Indiana to Portsmouth, Virginia in Day 12 of quarantine

WONDERFUL PEACE
W. D. Cornell W. G. Cooper

Far away in the depths of my spirit tonight
Rolls a melody sweeter than psalm;
In celestial-like strains it unceasingly falls,
O'er my soul like an infinite calm.

Peace! Peace! Wonderful Peace!
Coming down from the Father above,
Sweep over my spirit forever, I pray,
In the fathomless billows of love.

I am resting tonight in this wonderful peace,

Resting sweetly in Jesus' control;

For I'm kept from all danger

By night and by day,

And His glory is flooding my soul.

May 25, 2020, Monday

Indiana to Portsmouth, Virginia in Day 13 of the quarantine

Check out 'WHERE COULD I GO,' a J. B. COATS' SONG. You can find it on your i-phone. During the Civil War, Abraham Lincoln was asked how he was coping with all of the stress brought on by the war. It is said that he answered with "Where could I go, but to the Lord?"

May 26, 2020, Tuesday

Indiana to Portsmouth, Virginia Day 14 of the quarantine

(This song brings a lump to the throat--especially now that our country is suffering in every way.)

THE STAR-SPANGLED BANNER
FRANCIS SCOTT KEY

O, say, can you see, by the dawn's early light,
What so proudly we hailed
At the twilight's last gleaming?
Whose broad stripes and bright stars,
Through the perilous fight,
O'er the ramparts we watched,
Were so gallantly streaming?
And the rocket's red glare,
The bombs bursting in air,
Gave proof through the night
That our flag was still there.

O, say, does that Star-Spangled Banner yet wave
O'er the land of the free, and the home of the brave?

(It is a thrill to be down in the Baltimore Harbor on a foggy morning and look up at Ft. McHenry to see the flag waving and be inspired by the song written by Francis Scott Key.)

May 27, 2020, Wednesday

Indiana to Portsmouth, Virginia for Day 15 of quarantine

While you are waiting for the COVID-19 double test results, take a moment for this one—it seems that everyone in the Christian faith and those who are not, love this hymn. Someone can start singing it in a crowded area and everyone joins in.

AMAZING GRACE

John Newton Arr. E.O. Excell

Amazing grace!
How sweet the sound,
That saved a wretch like me!
I once was lost, but now am found,
Was blind, but now I see.

'Twas grace that taught my heart to fear,
And grace my fears relieved;
How precious did that grace appear
The hour I first believed!

Thro' many dangers, toils and snares,
I have already come;

'Tis grace hath bro't me safe this far,
And grace will lead me home.

When we've been there ten-thousand years,
Bright shining as the sun,
We've no less days to sing God's praise
Than when we first begun.

May 28, 2020, Friday
Indiana

Home!

BACK HOME AGAIN IN INDIANA
James F. Hanley and Ballard MacDonald (1917)

(You will want to pull this one up on your i-phone. I like the Jim Nabors recording.
While the words of this song have not really evoked memories for listeners of the past two generations, they are words that your grandparents actually lived. Young Grandpa put up 'fresh mown hay'. And I recall three

cuttings of hay each summer. Plus, your grandparents went to undergraduate college on the banks of the Wabash.)

By mid to late June the delayed funerals were held for some of the ones who died in the early months of the pandemic. At one funeral I found this hymn appropriately reflecting what needed to be said. (At that time, little did we know that we would be actively fighting this virus for more than another year before we could feel any measure of normalcy.)

O, THAT WILL BE GLORY
C.H.G. CHARLES H. GABRIEL
1900
When all my labors and trials are o'er,
And I am safe on that beautiful shore,
Just to be near the dear Lord I adore,
Will through the ages be glory for me.

When, by the gift of His infinite grace,
I am accorded in heaven a place,
Just to be there and to look on His face,
Will through the ages be glory for me.

Friends will be there I have loved long ago;
Joy like a river around me will flow;

Yet, just a smile from my Savior, I know,

Will through the ages be glory for me

June 28, 2020, Sunday

Indiana

JESUS IS ALL THE WORLD TO ME

W. L. T. W. L. THOMPSON

Jesus is all the world to me,

My life, my joy, my all;

He is my strength from day to day,

Without Him I would fall.

When I am sad, to Him I go,

No other one can cheer me so;

When I am sad

He makes me glad,

He's my friend.

Jesus is all the world to me,

My friend in trial sore;

I go to Him for blessings,

And He gives them o'er and o'er.

He sends the harvest's golden grain;
Sunshine and rain,
Harvest of grain,
He's my friend.

Jesus is all the world to me,
And true to Him I'll be;
O how could I this Friend deny,
When He's so true to me?
Following Him I know I'm right,
He watches o'er me day and night;
Following Him, by day and night,
He's my friend.

Jesus is all the world to me,
I want no better friend;
I trust Him now,
I'll trust Him when
Life's fleeting days shall end.
Beautiful life with such a friend;
Beautiful life that has no end;
Eternal life, eternal joy,
He's my friend.

EPILOGUE

Faith-building has been our theme. An underlying dialogue has been faith-building through the generations. Now for your own faith-building, let's draw from my story to make a list of ways my faith was/is building. The steps and principles for faith-building stand the test of time. I will start listing from what bolstered me in my own faith-journey and move through the decades to the present.

Now using these faith-builders and others, you can look at your own arsenal of faith for whatever may come in your own life. While it may seem that your trial is greater than you can bear, you can be prepared with God's help for the day-to-day trials as well as the years-long hardship.

You will know that God is able and your faith is in him. You can know who he is and what he has promised he will do. The requirement on your part is to talk with him telling him you believe what he did for you on the cross and asking him to forgive the sin in your life. Then let the faith-building begin:

1. Start where you are. Embracing meaningful lines of songs, a high school poem, wise sayings from elders and teachers at Bible school, camp and Sunday School.
2. Mining the gold out of the knowledge that 'Jesus loves you.'
3. Journaling, even when the entries are mere scribbles.
4. Drawing from the family tree those who exhibited a strong faith and get to know that person from afar or in person.
5. Mining for gold in Psalm 139 and II Corinthians 5:7
6. Having regular attendance in a local church, *repeatedly hearing* the words of the Bible, the words of the hymns, the prayers.
7. Joining a Bible Study requiring regular preparation.
8. Walking and talking with God just like you would walk and talk with your friend.

9. Let God be God leaving pettiness and vengeance to him, as he directed.

10. Let the hymns be guides of the faithful speaking to our present day

11. Do not worry if you have scars from your trials. Scars are your 'badges of courage.'

12. Do rest. Let your partner in the yoke help you carry your trials and troubles. He is able and wants to let you rest.

BIBLIOGRAPHY

Unless otherwise noted, all Scripture comes from the New Living Translation (NLT) of the Holy Bible, Tyndale House Publishers, Carol Stream, Illinois.

Ashley, A. H., 'He Lives,' copyright 1961. Renewal. The Rodehaver Company (Word Music, Waco, Texas). All rights reserved. #264. *Worship His* Majesty. Gaither Music Company. Alexandria, Indiana 1987.

From Munster Gesangbuch. 'Fairest Lord Jesus' Public Domain. Silesian Folk Melody. #188. *Worship His Majesty.* Gaither Music Co. Alexandria, Indiana. 1987.

Babcock, Maltbie D. and Sheppard, Franklin L., *'This is my Father's World,'* Public Domain. #73. *Worship His Majesty.* Gaither Music Company. Alexandria, Indiana. 1987.

Banta, Bruce, Black Mountain Conference Center, Fellowship of Christian Athletes Conference, 1982.

Baker, Theodore, translator and Kremser, Edward, harmonizer, 'We Gather Together.' Public Domain. Folk song of the Netherlands. #81. *Worship His Majesty*. Gaither Music Company. Alexandria, Indiana. 1987.

Baring-Gould, Sabine and Sullivan, Arthur, '*Onward Christian Soldiers*,' Public Domain. #600. *Worship His Majesty*. Gaither Music Company. Alexandria, Indiana. 1987.

Bartlett, E.M., 'Victory in Jesus,' copyright 1937. Renewal 1967. Extended by Mrs. E.M. Bartlett, Assigned to Albert E. Brumley and Sons. P.O. Box 27, Powell, Missouri 65730. #430. *Worship His Majesty*. Gaither Music Company. Alexandria, Indiana. 1987.

Bliss, P.P. '*Let The Lower Lights Be Burning*,' Public Domain. #395.*The American Service Hymnal. John Benson Publishing Company. Nashville, Tennessee. 1968.*

Chisholm, T.O. and Runyon, William M., 'Great Is Thy Faithfulness,' copyright 1923. Renewal 1951 by W.M. Runyon. Assigned to Hope Publishing Company. All rights reserved. #519. *Worship His Majesty*, Gaither Music Company. Alexandria, Indiana. 1987.

Clephane, Elizabeth C. and Maker, Frederick C., *'Beneath the Cross of Jesus,'* Public Domain. #226. *Worship His Majesty*. Gaither Music Company. 1987.

Coats, J. B., 'Where Could I Go,' copyright 1940. Stamps-Baxter Company in 'Golden Key.' (Now Zondervan Music Group.www.zondervan.com.) *Worship His Majesty*. Gaither Music Company. Alexandria, Indiana 1987.

Cornwell, W. D. and Cooper, W. G., *'Wonderful Peace,'* Public Domain. *#527. Worship His Majesty*. Gaither Music Company. Alexandria, Indiana. 1987.

Cowper, William and Mason, Lowell, *'There Is A Fountain,'* Public Domain. #253. *Worship His Majesty*. Gaither Music Company, Alexandria, Indiana. 1987.

Crosby, Fanny and Mrs. J. F. Knapp, 'Blessed Assurance,' Public Domain. #416. *Worship His Majesty*. Gaither Music Company. Alexandria, Indiana 1987.

Crosby, Fanny and Doane, William H., 'Rescue the Perishing,' Public Domain. #683. *Worship His Majesty. Gaither Music Company. 1987.*

Crosby, Fanny and Doane, William H., 'I Am Thine, O Lord,' Public Domain. #383. *Worship His Majesty.* Gaither Music Company. Alexandria, Indiana 1987.

Crouch, Andre, 'My Tribute,' copyright 1971. Lexicon Music Inc. Newberry Park, California. All rights reserved. #79. *Worship His Majesty.* Gaither Music Company. Alexandria, Indiana. 1987.

Cushing, William O. and Sankey, Ira D., 'Under His Wings,' Public Domain. #357. *Worship His Majesty.* Gaither Music Company. Alexandria, Indiana. 1987.

Dorsey, Thomas A., 'Take My Hand, Precious Lord,' copyright 1938. Assigned 1957 to Hill and Range Songs Inc. All rights reserved. #141. *The American Service Hymnal. John Benson Publishing Company. Nashville, Tennessee. 1968.*

Farjeon, Eleanor and Islam Yusuf, 'Morning Has Broken,' David Higham Associates.www.davidhigman.co.uk/

permission.1931. #74. *Worship His Majesty.* Gaither Music Company. Alexandria, Indiana 1987.

Gabriel, Charles, '*O That Will Be Glory for Me*,' Public Domain. #688. *Worship His Majesty,* Gaither Music Company. Alexandria, Indiana. 1987.

Gabriel, Charles, '*Send the Light*,' Public Domain. #672. *Worship His Majesty.* Gaither Music Company. Alexandria, Indiana. 1987.

Gaither, Gloria and William Gaither, '*Because He Lives*,' Copyright 1971. William J. Gaither. #260. *Worship His Majesty.* Gaither Music Company, Alexandria, Indiana. 1987. Used by permission.

Gaither, Gloria, William Gaither and Danny Daniels, '*I've Just Seen Jesus*,' Copyright 1984. Gaither Music Company and Ariose Music. #257. *Worship His Majesty.* Gaither Music Company, Alexandria, Indiana 1987. Used by permission.

Gaither, William, '*He Touched Me*,' Copyright 1963. #632. '*Worship His Majesty,*' Gaither Music Company, Alexandria, Indiana. 1987. Used by permission.

Graeff, Frank E. and Hall, J. Lincoln, *'Does Jesus Care?'* Public Domain.1901. #517.*Worship His Majesty*, Gaither Music Company. Alexandria, Indiana. 1987.

Howard B. Grose and Barnard, Charlotte A., *'Give of Your Best to the Master,'* Public Domain. <u>https://hymnary.org</u>. #591. *Worship His Majesty*. Gaither Music Company. Alexandria, Indiana 1987.

Hanley, James and Ballard MacDonald. *'Back Home Again in Indiana,'* 1917. Paull-Pioneer Music Corp. www, musixmatch.com.

Havergal, Frances R. and MaLan, C.H.A., *'Take My Life and Let It Be Consecrated,'*1874. Public Domain. #380. *Worship His Majesty. Gaither Music Company. Alexandria, Indiana. 1987.*

Hawthorne, Alice, *'Whispering Hope,'* Public Domain. #246. *The American Service Hymnal.* John Benson Publishing Company. Nashville, Tennessee. 1968.

Hewitt, Eliza E. and Sweeney, John R., *'Will There Be Any Stars in my Crown,'* Public Domain. #157. The American Service Hymnal. John Benson Publishing Company. Nashville, Tennessee. 1968.

Hoffman, E. H. and Stockton, J. H., 'Glory To His Name,' Public Domain. #444. The American Service Hymnal. John Benson Publishing Company. Nashville, Tennessee. 1968.

Indianapolis Star, Indianapolis, Indiana, August 24, 2020. Quote from Methodist Hospital nurse.

Irion, Mary Jean, 'Normal Day' Yes, World: A Mosaic of Meditation. R. W. Baron Publishing Company. 1970.

Jones, Ruth Caye, 'In Times Like These,' Copyright 1944 by Zondervan Music Publishers. All rights reserved. Used by permission. #114.The American Service Hymnal. John Benson Publishing Company. Nashville, Tennessee. 1968.

Key, Francis Scott, 'The Star-Spangled Banner,' Public Domain. #607. Worship His Majesty. Gaither Music Company. Alexandria, Indiana 1987.

MacLellan, Gene, 'Put Your Hand In The Hand,' Sony/ATV Music Publisher, LLC, 424 Church Street, Suite 1200, Nashville, Tennessee 37219. humanresource@sonymusicpub.com.

Martin, W. C. and Miles, C. Austin, 'Still Sweeter Every Day,' Public Domain. #190. The American Service Hymnal. John Benson Publishing Company. Nashville, Tennessee. 1968.

Miles, C. Austin, (CAM), 'In the Garden,' copyright 1940. Renewal Rodeheaver Co. Inc. (Word Music, P.O. Box 1790, Waco, Texas 76796) Used by permission. #270. *Worship His Majesty.* Gaither Music Company. Alexandria, Indiana. *1987.*

Lehman, F.M., *'The Love of God,'* copyright 1917. Renewal 1945 by Nazarene Publishing House. Kansas City, Missouri. #96. *Worship His Majesty.* Gaither Music Company. Alexandria, Indiana. 1987.

Lemmel, Helen Howard, *'Turn Your Eyes Upon Jesus,'* Copyright 1922. Renewal 1950. H.H. Lemmel. Assigned to Singspiration, Inc./Zondervan Publishing. All rights reserved. #491.*Worship His Majesty.* Gaither Music Company. Alexandria, Indiana 1987.

Lowry, Robert, *'Christ Arose,'* Public Domain. #256. *Worship His Majesty.* Gaither Music Company. Alexandria, Indiana 1987.

Kirkpatrick William James and John Thomas McFarland, *'Away in a Manger,'* 1895.Public Domain. #129. *Worship His Majesty.* Gaither Music Company. Alexandria, Indiana 1987.

Lytle, H. F. and Mone, W. H., *'Abide With Me,'* Public Domain. #528. *Worship His Majesty.* Gaither Music Company. Alexandria, Indiana 1987.

Newton, John, *'Amazing Grace'* Public Domain. Arr. E. O. Excell. *#429.Worship His Majesty.* Gaither Music Company. Alexandria, Indiana. 1987.

Nicholson, James and Fischer, William G. *'Whiter Than Snow,'* Public Domain. #476. *Worship His Majesty.* Gaither Music Company. Alexandria, Indiana. 1987.

Oatman, Johnson, Jr. and Gabriel, Charles H., *'Higher Ground,'* Public Domain. #401.*Worship His Majesty.* Gaither Music Company. Alexandria, Indiana. 1987.

Oatman, Johnson, Jr.and Hugg, George C., *'No Not One,'* Public Domain. #222. *The American Service Hymnal.* John Benson Publishing Company. Nashville, Tennessee. 1968.

Rankin, J. E. and Tomer, W. G., 'God Be with You,' Public Domain. #323.Worship His Majesty. Gaither Music Company, Alexandria, Indiana. 1987.

"Redwoods Still Standing After Inferno," USAToday, Gannett Newspapers. August 24, 2020

Reed, Jerry, 'A Thing Called Love,' Mojo Music and Media, 437 E. Iris Drive, Nashville, Tennessee 37204. mojomusicandmedia.com.

Rowley, Frances and Bilhorn, Peter Philip, 'I Will Sing the Wondrous Story,' Public Domain. #652.Worship His Majesty. Gaither Music Company. Alexandria, Indiana. 1987.

Robinson, Robert and Wyeth, John, 'Come Thou Fount,' Public Domain. # 30. Worship His Majesty. Gaither Music Company. Alexandria, Indiana 1987.

Roland, Tom, 'What I'm Leavin' For,' Universal Music Publishing Group, Nashville, Tennessee.

Sergel, J.B. and Austris A. Witol, 'My God and I' New Spring, Inc, administered by Brentwood-Benson Publishing Company, Nashville, Tennessee.

Steinbeck, John, 'The Moon Is Down,' 1942. Viking Press, New York.

Stevens, W. B. and arr. J.R. Baxter, Jr., *Farther Along,* 1937. Zondervan Music Group. 365 Great Circle Drive. Nashville, Tennessee 37228. #243 The American Service Hymnal. John Benson Publishing. Nashville, Tennessee. 1968.

Stevenson, Robert Louis, 'Consolation,' Underwoods : A Collection of Poems. 1892.Mathuen Publishing Company. North Yorkshire, England.

Thompson, W. L., *'Jesus Is All the World to Me,'* Public Domain. #635. *Worship His Majesty.* Gaither Music Company, Alexandria, Indiana. 1987.

Watts, Isaac and Mason, Lowell, *'When I Survey the Wondrous Cross,'* Public Domain. #225. *Worship His Majesty. Gaither Music Company. Alexandria, Indiana 1987.*

Willis, Wallace, *'Swing Low'* African Spiritual. *The Jubilee Singers,* 1873. www.lyricfind.com.

Yates, John G. and Stanley, Ira D., *'Faith is the Victory,'* Public Domain. #432. *Worship His Majesty.* Gaither Music Company. Alexandria, Indiana. 1987.

Zelley, Rev. H. J. and Cook, G. H., *'Heavenly Sunlight,'* Public Domain. #167. The American Service Hymnal. John Benson Publishing Company. Nashville, Tennessee. 1968.

Lightning Source UK Ltd.
Milton Keynes UK
UKHW012015070921
390207UK00001B/15